D1571831

Between the Sheets

Between the Sheets
by Jordi Mand

Playwrights Canada Press
Toronto

Between the Sheets © 2014 by Jordi Mand

For professional or amateur production rights, please contact:
Ian Arnold at Catalyst Talent Creative Management
310-100 Broadview Ave., Toronto, ON M4M 3H3
416.645.0935, info@catalysttcm.com

LIBRARY AND ARCHIVES CANADA CATALOGUING IN PUBLICATION
Mand, Jordi, author
    Between the sheets / Jordi Mand.

A play.
Issued in print and electronic formats.
ISBN 978-1-77091-210-6 (pbk.).--ISBN 978-1-77091-211-3 (pdf).--
ISBN 978-1-77091-212-0 (epub)

    I. Title.

PS8626.A519B48 2013   C812'.6   C2013-908001-5
                                 C2013-908002-3

We acknowledge the financial support of the Canada Council for the Arts, the Ontario Arts Council (OAC)—an agency of the Government of Ontario, which last year funded 1,681 individual artists and 1,125 organizations in 216 communities across Ontario for a total of $52.8 million—the Ontario Media Development Corporation, and the Government of Canada through the Canada Book Fund for our publishing activities.

 Canada Council Conseil des arts
for the Arts du Canada

 ONTARIO ARTS COUNCIL
CONSEIL DES ARTS DE L'ONTARIO
50 YEARS OF ONTARIO GOVERNMENT SUPPORT OF THE ARTS
50 ANS DE SOUTIEN DU GOUVERNEMENT DE L'ONTARIO AUX ARTS

 Canada

 Ontario
Ontario Media Development
Corporation

Between the Sheets was first produced by Nightwood Theatre from September 18 to October 7, 2012, in the Tarragon Theatre Extra Space, Toronto. It featured the following cast and creative team:

Marion: Susan Coyne
Teresa: Christine Horne

Directed by Kelly Thornton
Dramaturgy by Erica Kopyto
Set and costume design by Kelly Wolf
Lighting design by Bonnie Beecher
Music and sound design by Richard Feren

Between the Sheets was first developed as part of Nightwood Theatre's Write From the Hip Program from February 2010 to February 2011. The play received a public reading with the same cast and director as above.

Between the Sheets received a workshop production as part of Nightwood Theatre's New Groundswell Festival in November of 2011 with the same cast as above. It featured the following creative team:

Directed by Kelly Thornton
Dramaturgy by Erica Kopyto
Set and costume design by Camellia Koo
Lighting design by Sandra Henderson
Music and sound design by Richard Feren

Characters

Teresa
Marion

An elementary school classroom.

The room is filled with colourful class projects. Small desks and chairs are set up neatly in rows. The words "Parent Teacher Interviews" are written on the blackboard. Pieces of decorated construction paper hang from the front of every desk with a student's name on it. There is a garbage can near the front desk. The room is spacious but intimate.

We see TERESA in her class. She is in her late twenties. She wears a warm-coloured dress, tights, shoes with a bit of a heel, and a thin gold necklace. There is a sweater draped over the back of her chair. She is naturally beautiful and wears very little makeup.

TERESA is tidying the room, repositioning some of the chairs and desks. There are two chairs set up at the front of the class where parents have sat. She moves them to the back of the class.

She walks to the blackboard, grabs an eraser, and wipes the board clean. There are a few piles of file folders neatly stacked on the corner of her desk. She puts them into a filing cabinet. She returns to her desk and takes a long sip from a mug.

She moves a few more things around. As she does, she knocks some papers to the floor.

TERESA   Shit.

TERESA gets up out of her chair to clean the mess.

Beat.

As she picks up the last piece of paper from the floor she stands and sees MARION in the doorway.

MARION is in her early fifties. She wears a tailored grey suit with a crisp white blouse. She carries a large purse over one shoulder and drapes a coat over her arms. She wears pearl earrings and a diamond wedding band. She is meticulous about her appearance.

TERESA and MARION stare at one another.

MARION   Miss Stewart?

Beat.

TERESA   Yes.

Beat.

MARION   I'm Alex's mother.

TERESA   Of course.

MARION   I hope I'm not too late. I got held up at the office.

TERESA   Late?

MARION   For the interviews. They're tonight, are they not?

TERESA   They are but... I just held my last one.

MARION   Oh.

TERESA   I was just finishing up, actually.

MARION   Well I'm sure you wouldn't mind if I grabbed the last slot then.

          MARION enters the room.

          I just have a few quick questions for you about Alex... about his report card.

          MARION goes to close the door.

TERESA   Leave it open.

          MARION looks at her.

          If you don't mind... it's school policy.

MARION   It's school policy to keep the door open?

TERESA   During school hours, yes.

MARION   But your students aren't here.

TERESA   It's still considered school hours… please.

> *Beat.*

MARION   Well… it's your class.

> *MARION smiles.*

> *TERESA tentatively smiles back.*

> *Beat.*

> *MARION goes to place her coat and purse on one of the student's chairs. She pulls out a leather binder and glasses case from her purse.*

> *She walks towards TERESA's desk.*

Where would you like me to…

TERESA   Oh.

> *TERESA goes to get a chair for her.*

I apologize. I'm a bit tired. It's been a long day.

MARION   Well, I won't keep you long.

TERESA   Thank you. I would appreciate that.

*TERESA pulls up a chair for MARION, placing it fairly far
from the teacher's desk.*

MARION sits.

*TERESA takes a sip of water from the mug and then sits
behind her desk.*

*MARION notices how far she has been placed from TERESA
and shimmies her chair towards the desk.*

MARION   So?

TERESA   So.

MARION   Do I just ask you my questions or... how do you normally
like to start these things, Miss Stewart?

TERESA   Yes. Please. Ask your questions. My preference is always
for parents to ask their questions first.

MARION   You're sure?

TERESA   Yes. Please... go ahead.

Beat.

MARION   All right.

*MARION takes her glasses out of the case. She opens her
binder.*

TERESA stands and walks to the filing cabinet. She pulls out a folder.

What is that?

TERESA   Alex's file.

MARION   His file?

TERESA   I have a file for all of my students. I keep track of past reports, academic history—

MARION   You're very organized.

TERESA   You have to be.

MARION   It helps, doesn't it?

TERESA   What?

MARION   Being organized. Knowing where everything is. Knowing how to find everything that's yours.

TERESA   Yes. I suppose it does.

Beat.

MARION   I have been looking over Alex's report card…

MARION holds up the report card.

There's a noticeable difference from the start of the year.

TERESA   There is.

MARION   His math mark especially.

TERESA   Alex has been making tremendous progress.

MARION   I can see that.

TERESA   It's been a real pleasure having him in my class. He's quite the character.

MARION   I'm glad to see that he's understanding the material.

TERESA   I've noticed a real improvement over the past few—

MARION   His English mark is low… still.

TERESA   He's come a long way in English, actually. He wrote a fantastic book report last month. He got up and presented it in front of the whole class. I asked for a few volunteers and he jumped at the opportunity.

MARION   Was he marked on that?

TERESA   Marked?

MARION   Was he marked on his presentation in front of the class?

TERESA   It wasn't really a presentation. I asked for a few volunteers to—

MARION   What does that have to do with his English mark then?

TERESA   He's making progress. He wouldn't have done something
           like that at the start of the year. He wouldn't have stood
           in front of the class and read something he worked on…
           something he wrote. That was a big step for him.

MARION   That may be but his mark is still low.

TERESA   It's higher then it was last term.

           TERESA opens the folder.

MARION   How is he doing compared to the rest of the class?

TERESA   I try not to compare my students.

MARION   Really? You don't compare them?

TERESA   No.

MARION   I think that's a bit impossible.

TERESA   It's not, actually.

MARION   Every time you give them a mark, you're seeing one student
           get one grade and one student get another. They're being
           compared to one another whether you like it or not.

TERESA   That may be but I don't go out of my way to… I just find
           it isn't a constructive way to teach.

MARION   It's constructive for them. It helps them know who's ahead
           and who's falling behind. Who's at the top of the class,
           who's—

TERESA   I try not to put too much emphasis on their marks. I want them to feel—

MARION   Their marks determine everything for them.

TERESA   What and how they learn determines—

MARION   You think universities—

TERESA   I think it's a little early to be thinking about university.

MARION   It's never too early.

TERESA   They're in grade three.

MARION   It's never too early!

TERESA grabs a tissue from the box on her desk. She smiles.

What?

TERESA   No, it's just…

TERESA gently pats her forehead with the tissue.

You're the third parent today to mention university.

MARION   Well that's what we're paying for here… isn't it?

Beat.

TERESA throws the tissue in the garbage.

TERESA   I understand the need to be concerned about their marks. I do. But they're young and they're going to be students for a long time. They have years ahead of them where all they'll be asked to think about is their marks.

I'm trying to encourage them to take the time now... while they can... to understand how they learn. To understand what their strengths are, what their weakness are. What their—

MARION   How long have you been teaching?

TERESA   Why?

MARION   I'd like to know a bit about the woman who's teaching my son, if that's all right?

TERESA   It's my second year.

MARION   Second year teaching or second year—

TERESA   It's my second year here.

MARION   Were you teaching before this?

TERESA   Yes. At Westview.

MARION   I've never heard of it.

TERESA   It's north. It's a smaller school.

MARION   And how long were you there for?

TERESA   Two years.

MARION   Why did you move here?

TERESA   I had wanted to teach here since I graduated.

MARION   And you managed to sneak your way in?

TERESA   I didn't sneak my way into anything. It's quite difficult to
           find a position at a school like this.

MARION   I'm sure there are all kinds of positions out there for—

TERESA   There aren't. I know people who've been on a waiting list
           for years… and that's just to supply. Some of my classmates
           are serving tables just to—

MARION   Well, you're young. I'm sure—

TERESA   I'm not that young.

MARION   No? You look it.

> *TERESA accidentally knocks her pencil off the desk. She
> begins to search for it. As she does, MARION reaches to the
> floor and grabs it.*
>
> *MARION looks at TERESA and extends her arm to offer the
> pencil. TERESA takes it from her.*

TERESA   Thanks.

> *They look at one another for a moment.*

Mrs. Siller, do you...

MARION   Do I...

Beat.

TERESA   Do you have any more questions? About Alex, perhaps... about his report card?

MARION looks at her.

MARION   No. No, I think I've taken up enough of your time.

MARION stands and places her binder on the desk. She puts her glasses back in the case. She walks to the back of the room to collect her things.

I appreciate you sneaking me in, Miss Stewart. I know it's been a long day.

TERESA   It's my pleasure.

MARION   I'm sure.

TERESA notices MARION's binder on her desk.

TERESA   You forgot your—

MARION   It's funny though...

Beat.

You seemed surprised to see me.

Beat.

TERESA   Surprised?

Beat.

MARION   Yes. When I first walked in. You seemed... surprised.

TERESA   I just wasn't expecting you.

MARION   Why? Because we didn't have a time slot?

TERESA   You had a time slot.

MARION   No, I don't think we did. That's why I tried to catch you at the end of the day.

TERESA   Everyone received a time slot.

MARION   I'm telling you—

TERESA   I was told you wouldn't be coming.

MARION   You were?

TERESA   Yes. That neither you or your husband would be coming this term.

MARION   And... who told you that?

TERESA   Alex.

MARION   How would Alex know whether we were coming or not? That's not something we would discuss with him.

TERESA   Sometimes the only way I know if parents are coming is if their child lets me know.

MARION   You should have checked with one of us.

TERESA   I did.

MARION   You didn't check with me.

TERESA   No. I checked with your husband.

MARION   With my husband?

TERESA   Yes. He was picking Alex up one afternoon so I asked him to confirm... he said that the two of you knew about the interviews but wouldn't be coming.

MARION   You said Alex told you.

TERESA   Alex told me initially but I checked—

MARION   With my husband. Yes and... when was this?

TERESA   When?

MARION   Yes. When did you check with him?

TERESA   About a week ago.

MARION   So... last week?

TERESA   I believe so, yes.

          Beat.

MARION   Tell me... why is it that my husband seems to be the only one receiving information from you?

TERESA   I don't believe that's true.

MARION   No? You said that my husband knew about the interviews. Why wasn't I informed?

TERESA   I don't know.

MARION   You don't. You don't have any idea?

TERESA   I left a message on your house line.

MARION   I never received any message from you.

TERESA   Well, I left one. School policy is that we phone parents... all parents... to let them know about these types of events. I—

          TERESA walks back to her desk. She rifles through the pages in Alex's folder.

          932-7674. Is that your home number?

MARION   Yes.

TERESA   I left a message on that line.

MARION   This isn't the first time that this has happened. My husband knew about the museum trip last month that he volunteered for. I didn't know about that little excursion either. I didn't know anything about it until Alex mentioned it that morning.

TERESA   I phoned your house on that occasion as well. As you can appreciate, it's very hard for me to know how information is being disseminated. I have no way of knowing who's—

MARION   Does the school know you're only keeping in touch with one of Alex's parents?

TERESA   It's quite common.

MARION   Is it?

TERESA   Absolutely. I often only have contact with one parent per household during the school year.

MARION   Alex has been here for three years. That's never been our experience.

TERESA   As you know, parents are very busy. It isn't unusual for one parent to take the lead with class communication.

MARION   Class communication?

TERESA   How I communicate what's happening—

MARION   I understand what it means, thanks.

MARION drops her coat and purse on one of the student's desks.

And how is that decision made exactly?

TERESA How?

MARION Yes. How do you determine which parent in any given household you're going to communicate with?

TERESA It can depend.

MARION On?

TERESA On a number of things. If a parent has requested to—

MARION Did one of us request that? I certainly didn't, so unless a decision was made without my consent—

TERESA Your husband asked me to be in touch regarding Alex's school year. I'm not privy to how those decisions are made at home.

MARION He asked you that? He asked you not to contact me?

TERESA He didn't ask me not to contact you. He simply asked me to contact him. There's a difference.

MARION Apparently.

TERESA Again, I don't know how those decisions are made. I simply contact whoever—

MARION Well you've been doing an excellent job then, don't you think?

Beat.

TERESA   Excuse me?

MARION   You heard me.

TERESA   I don't know what you mean by—

MARION   I think you do.

         Beat.

         I've seen you.

TERESA   Seen?

MARION   Together… in the parking lot.

TERESA   I don't know what you're talking about—

MARION   We came to pick up Alex. I went to the office to drop something off. I saw the two of you talking to one another. He leaned in to whisper something to you. He put his hand on your back. Do you not remember that?

TERESA   I don't. I think you…

MARION   You think what?

TERESA   I think you have the wrong idea.

MARION   No. No, I don't think I do.

TERESA   Mrs. Siller—

MARION   What!?

        Beat.

TERESA   I want you to know… I hear what you're saying. I hear your frustration.

MARION   Do you?

TERESA   Yes. You feel like, perhaps, you haven't been kept in the loop as much as you would like regarding what takes place in my class.

MARION   I think I've been deliberately kept out of the loop, Miss Stewart.

TERESA   I can assure you… no one is keeping you out of anything.

MARION   I don't believe that.

TERESA   No one is—

MARION   I don't believe that for one fucking second.

TERESA   Please, just… calm down.

MARION   Don't tell me to calm down. I know what I saw!

TERESA   Look…

        Beat.

I thought your husband was passing along everything we spoke about regarding Alex's school year. I can be in touch with you on a more regular basis, if you prefer. That's not a problem. We can—

MARION   Do you understand what I'm saying to you or not?

TERESA   I understand what you're implying.

MARION   Implying?

TERESA   I'm not sure why you have it in your head that—

MARION   You think I'm making this up?

TERESA   I didn't say—

MARION   You look me in the eye and tell me that I'm making this up.

> TERESA *looks at her.*

TERESA   I think you're confused.

MARION   Confused?

TERESA   I think there's been some confusion around what you think you saw.

MARION   You sent home notes with my son.

TERESA   I send notes home with all of my students.

MARION   You sent a note home… after Parents' Night… at the start
           of the year. I found it in Alex's bag. You gave my husband
           your email address.

TERESA   He asked for a way to contact me. He had a few questions
           regarding the curriculum—

MARION   It was your personal email address.

TERESA   I give out both of my accounts. It depends on—

MARION   What? It depends on what?

TERESA   Our school accounts are temperamental. If someone needs
           to get in touch with me… it isn't uncommon for me to give
           out my personal account.

MARION   And the school is aware of the fact that you ask parents to
           contact you at home?

TERESA   I have never asked anyone to contact me at home, per se.

MARION   You asked my husband. "Be in touch." You wrote that on a
           note you sent home with Alex. You wrote that beside your
           personal email address.

TERESA   Your husband had some questions about the first unit we
           were working on.

MARION   Not once this entire year have you reached out to me and
           yet you gave—

TERESA   Mrs. Siller... with all due respect... we are halfway
         through the school year.

MARION   I'm aware of that.

TERESA   If there was a problem you've had every opportunity to
         approach me. You could have let me know that you weren't
         happy with the way we were—

MARION   Well I'm telling you now.

TERESA   Exactly. I have left countless messages at your house this
         year. I have sent home class reports... permission forms
         for class trips. This is the first time it has been brought to
         my attention that there is any kind of problem.

MARION   Stop it.

TERESA   If you have had an issue with the way I was communicat-
         ing with you or your husband you could have come to me
         sooner—

MARION   You can't keep doing this. You're lying.

TERESA   I never—

MARION   You have been writing to him for months. You have been
         writing to each other for months.

TERESA   I told you—

MARION   You didn't have to do that. You didn't have to write to him.
         You didn't have to tempt him.

TERESA   Tempt him?

MARION   Yes! You tempted him! You tempted my husband!

> *MARION grabs her binder and slams it open on TERESA's desk.*

Read it.

> *Beat.*

(quietly) Read it!

> *TERESA hesitates then moves towards her desk.*

> *She reads the page that lies open in the binder.*

I have every one… every single one. Every one you wrote to him. Every one he wrote to you.

> *TERESA begins to flip through the pages in the binder.*

TERESA   Where…

> *She takes a moment.*

(quietly) Where did you get these from? These are—

MARION   What? These are—

TERESA   *(quietly)* Private!

> *TERESA closes the binder.*

It's none of your business.

MARION   All of this is my business! I have the right to know everything that's been going on between the two of you.

TERESA   Where did you—

MARION   Does the school know this is the kind of contact you have with parents here?

TERESA   I don't have contact with any other parents—

MARION   No, that's right… you only have contact with my husband.

TERESA   Does he know you have these?

MARION   Does that matter?

TERESA   Yes! It's a crime… you know that, don't you?

MARION   A crime?

TERESA   Breaking into his… entering someone else's—

MARION   I didn't enter anything, you little shit. He left his account open. On our computer! In our office! At our home!

TERESA heads for the door.

Where are you going—

TERESA closes it.

TERESA   I understand that you're upset.

MARION   You understand nothing.

TERESA   But I can't talk to you about this here. This is my job.

MARION   Well you should have thought about that before you—

TERESA   Please. Somebody could hear us. Somebody might walk in. I wouldn't do this to you. I wouldn't barge into your office—

MARION   You would have no business being at my office. I pay for my son to be here. Don't you forget that. I pay... we pay for our son to be in the same room with you every day. I have every right to be here.

TERESA   Please.

MARION   Do you think this is easy for me... to be in the same room as you?

TERESA   No. I don't. But you—

MARION   How long have you been seeing him?

        Beat.

        Answer the question.

TERESA   Marion.

MARION   Don't do that. Don't use my name.

TERESA walks to her desk.

TERESA   This has nothing to do with me.

MARION   It has nothing to do with you?

TERESA   This is between you and him.

MARION   How can you say that? It has everything to do with you.

TERESA   I—

MARION   You are fucking my husband!

> *TERESA goes to her purse. She pulls out her phone.*

What are you doing?

> *TERESA begins to dial. Her hands shake.*

Put that down.

> *TERESA turns away.*

I'm serious.

> *MARION moves closer to her.*

Put down the phone.

TERESA   *(into the phone)* Hi!

MARION grabs the phone out of TERESA's hand and throws it against the blackboard.

The phone shatters into pieces.

TERESA freezes.

MARION   I don't care if this is your job... I don't care if this is where you work. I will go to the principal, the parents' board... I don't care who I have to speak to. You will be out of here so fucking fast—

TERESA   This doesn't concern my job.

MARION   You better believe it concerns your job. You are sleeping with a student's father.

TERESA   ·They would have cause for concern if this involved a student but it doesn't.

MARION   You think the school wants to know that you're fucking—

TERESA   I am great at my job.

MARION   I don't care if you're the best goddamn teacher in the universe... I will make your life as difficult as I possibly can. Do you understand me?

TERESA   I—

MARION   How long have you been seeing him!?

Beat.

Answer the question or so help me god I will—

TERESA   A couple of months.

    Beat.

MARION   A couple?

TERESA   Yes. A couple.

MARION   So… what? Since December, January—

TERESA   Since Sept— Since the end of September.

    Beat.

MARION   Who else knows about this?

TERESA   No one.

MARION   You haven't told anyone?

TERESA   No.

MARION   You haven't told any of your girlfriends?

TERESA   No.

MARION   Family? Roommates? Co-workers? Does anyone here know?

TERESA   I said no!

MARION shakes her head in disbelief.

MARION   *(quietly)* He should have known better.

TERESA   He's—

MARION   He's old enough to be your father.

TERESA   He's not that old.

MARION   Oh, yes he is.

TERESA   Well… I'm not that young.

MARION   No?

TERESA   No.

MARION   How old *are* you?

TERESA   Twenty-eight.

MARION   Oh god.

MARION covers her face with her hands.

Beat.

She turns to TERESA.

When were you last together?

Beat.

I know it's been in the last week.

Beat.

Where do you meet?

Beat.

Where do you meet him?

TERESA   I have never been to your house, if that's what you're asking.

MARION   How do I know that? How do I know that you're telling the truth?

TERESA   I don't know how you know that.

MARION   · I want you to tell me.

TERESA   I am. I am telling you! What... what do you want me to say?

MARION   You stood there minutes ago and you lied to my face. How the hell am I supposed to—

TERESA   Why are you asking me anything if you're not going to believe me?

MARION   You have been deceiving me for months.

TERESA   I have not been deceiving you.

MARION   No?

TERESA   No! He...

She stops herself.

You should be talking to him.

MARION   I want to hear it from you.

TERESA   You should be asking—

MARION   I want to hear it from you. Where do you meet?

Beat.

Do you meet him here?

TERESA   What?

MARION   Do you meet my husband—

TERESA   No!

MARION   You're sure?

TERESA   Yes. I'm sure. I would never—

MARION   You would never what?

TERESA   I would never do something like that. This is my classroom. Why would you even ask me that?

MARION   Then where? In a hotel? In a car? On the street?

TERESA   At my apartment.

MARION   Your apartment.

TERESA   Yes.

MARION   Do you live alone?

TERESA   Yes. I live alone.

MARION   Does he have a key?

TERESA   No, he does not have a key.

MARION   How do you know when to meet? How does he know when
            to come over?

TERESA   I don't know. Look, we...

            She stops herself.

            We've only been together a few times.

MARION   What does that mean... a few times? You've only seen
            each other a few times? You've only fucked each other a
            few times?

TERESA   We've only slept together a few times... yes.

MARION   So... what? Twice? Three times?

TERESA   I haven't counted.

MARION   Do you use protection?

TERESA   What?

MARION   I need to know if I should be tested for—

TERESA   You don't need to be tested for anything.

MARION   Do you use protection or not?

TERESA   Yes.

MARION   What? Are you on birth control?

TERESA   No. I'm not on birth control.

MARION   No!

TERESA   No. We use condoms, all right?

MARION   Condoms?

TERESA   Yes.

MARION   Does he buy them or do you?

TERESA   I don't know.

MARION   So they just appear out of nowhere?

TERESA   No. He...

TERESA buries her head in her hands.

MARION   You're going to stop seeing him. Do you understand me? You're going to contact him tonight and you're going to tell him it's over. You're going to tell him it's over and then you are never to communicate with him again. You won't write to him… you won't call him—

TERESA   *(quietly)* It's not that simple.

MARION   Simple? What did you think was going to happen?

TERESA   I didn't think anything.

MARION   Well that's the problem, isn't it? You weren't thinking. Neither of you were thinking.

TERESA   We—

MARION   You think I don't know what he sees in you? You're young, you're attractive, you're some kind of answer.

TERESA   Answer?

MARION   Yes. You're the answer to his fucking mid-life crisis.

TERESA   You don't have to do that.

MARION   What?

TERESA   You don't have to make him sound like some kind of… he's not like that.

MARION   He's not like what… he's not like every other man his age?
          Sleeping with some young… he's twice your age, for fuck's
          sakes.

TERESA   Well you're the only one who seems to have a problem
          with that.

MARION   Problem? Sweetheart… do you not see what's going
          on here?

TERESA   He's—

MARION   He's using you. He wouldn't be doing this if he—

TERESA   He wouldn't be doing this if he didn't have feelings for me.

MARION   Feelings? Do you hear yourself?

TERESA   You have no idea.

MARION   This is a phase.

TERESA   I'm sure it's easier for you to think that.

MARION   Believe me… nothing could possibly make this easier
          for me.

TERESA   No. It is. It's easier for you to think that this is a phase or
          some kind of an answer to—

MARION   It's an affair. You are having an—

TERESA   It's a relationship!

MARION laughs.

MARIÓN   Oh god.

She continues to laugh.

Oh dear god.

MARION looks at her.

He's married. You know that, don't you?

TERESA   Yes. I know that.

MARION   He is not single. He is not a bachelor. He is not available. The man you are talking about is my husband. Doesn't that mean anything to you?

TERESA   Of course it means something to me.

MARION   You can't just meet to fuck each other whenever—

TERESA   That's not what this is about. It's not—

MARION   It not what?

TERESA   It's not about sex.

MARION   It isn't?

TERESA   No.

MARION   You're sleeping with him... aren't you?

TERESA   That just happened.

MARION   You just happened to find yourself in bed with my husband?

TERESA   No.

MARION   How can you say it's not about sex?

TERESA   Look... it doesn't matter what I say to you, all right?
              Everything that comes out of my mouth is going to sound
              stupid or young or whatever it is you think I am. But this
              is real... this is real, and if he were here he would be telling
              you exactly the same thing.

MARION   He—

TERESA   Neither of us was looking for this. I knew he was married.
              Of course I knew he was married. But it's not as if I went
              out of my way to find a married man to sleep with. I hate
              the fact that he has a life with someone else... that he has
              a life with you.

              I know you think this is just about sex... and I get it. I do.
              But it's not and you need to know that. It has never been
              about that.

              MARION grabs the binder from TERESA's desk.

MARION   *(reading)* "I ache until I can hold you inside me again."

TERESA   Don't.

MARION   *(reading)* "Your sweat on my skin… the taste of you in my mouth…"

TERESA   Stop.

MARION   *(reading)* "The thought of you… the very thought of you makes me wet."

TERESA   Stop it.

MARION   It's not about sex?

TERESA   You don't understand.

MARION   Obviously I don't.

TERESA   He writes to me. He writes to me all the time.

MARION   Yes, I've been reading his work.

TERESA   No. You haven't read these. He's been writing short stories for me… poetry.

MARION   What… like assignments?

TERESA   You don't get it.

MARION   I get it. You're giving my husband homework.

TERESA   This is not a joke! You have no idea what he's written about… how much he's shared with me… how much I know about your life together.

MARION   What?

TERESA   I know about your first date... about your wedding night... about fights that you've had. I know you were sleeping in separate rooms for a while. I know about the last time you actually touched each other. He has shared some of the most private, intimate details of your marriage.

MARION   You have some fucking nerve.

MARION breathes heavily.

She moves away from TERESA.

TERESA follows her.

TERESA   He's miserable. He's told me, over and over again... how sad... how lonely he's felt... how trapped he's felt.

He's happy. For the first time in years he is actually—

MARION falls to her knees and vomits into the garbage can beside TERESA's desk.

TERESA backs away.

Beat.

TERESA goes to her desk and grabs a few tissues and her mug. She goes to MARION and offers her both.

Do you want some water or...

MARION takes the tissues from TERESA and wipes her face. She puts her arm out, indicating for TERESA to give her space.

TERESA places the mug on the desk and moves away from MARION.

MARION sits for a few moments and tries to steady her breathing.

She wipes her mouth and stands.

MARION takes a few moments. She takes a sip of water.

Beat.

She looks at TERESA.

MARION   I'm going to tell you something and I want you to listen because this is something he would never admit about himself.

Beat.

He is never satisfied.

MARION looks at TERESA.

He is never satisfied. And the reason he would never admit that is because… he doesn't know. He has no idea that he's been living his life this way… that for years he has been living his life this way. Whatever it is you think you've found together… in the end… it won't matter. He is never ever happy. And he never will be.

Beat.

MARION throws the tissue in the garbage.

MARION stands. She notices some of the projects hanging on the bulletin board. She stares at the board for a long time.

TERESA watches her.

TERESA   *(pointing to the board)* Alex's project is—

MARION   I know which project is his.

Beat.

MARION reaches out to touch one of the projects.

Does he know?

TERESA   What?

MARION   My son! Does my son know?

TERESA   No!

MARION   You're sure?

TERESA   Yes. I'm sure.

MARION   But he's seen the two of you together.

TERESA   Only when he's being dropped off or picked up.

MARION   Have you ever seen him outside of school?

TERESA   No.

MARION   After school, on the weekends… have you ever—

TERESA   I have never seen your son outside of this school!

> *MARION looks at her. She moves to get her coat and bag.*

MARION   I want him as far away from you as possible.

TERESA   What? Why?

MARION   Why? Because… you've put him in a dangerous situation.

TERESA   How is this dangerous?

MARION   Alex isn't safe in your class.

TERESA   My students' safety is the most important thing to me.
           I would never do anything to put any of my students in
           danger.

MARION   My son—

TERESA   Your son is doing well. Alex is having the best year he's
           had since he started here.

MARION   Of course he is. He's smart.

TERESA   You're right. He is smart. He's also... incredibly
              challenging.

MARION   Kids are challenging.

TERESA   Not like Alex. His teachers haven't always known how to
              work with him.

MARION   He's struggled a bit here and there.

TERESA   Struggled? Marion, he's been drowning.

              TERESA goes to get Alex's file.

              I have all of Alex's report cards since he started here. I
              have comment after comment from his teachers... each of
              them noting his behaviour as an issue. That he has trouble
              focusing... trouble staying on topic... that he zones out
              during class if he—

MARION   Every kid zones out. You try finding a kid that—

TERESA   No. Not every kid. Not like Alex. He used to talk to
              himself... he was continually disrupting the class—

MARION   Then you should be doing a better job of controlling them.
              It's your job to—

TERESA   It's because I have been doing my job... because Alex and
              I have been working together... creating a system together
              that he—

MARION   A system?

TERESA   Yes.

MARION   What system?

TERESA   So he can function. So he can stay focused in class.

MARION   What are you talking about?

TERESA   I've been giving him ways to help organize his thoughts. It's been good for him. He doesn't feel like his mind is moving a million miles per minute.

MARION   Does the school know you're using systems—

TERESA   Of course they know. I've consulted with a number of teachers here who—

MARION   What teachers?

TERESA   From the resource program.

MARION   The resource program?

TERESA   Yes. Alex's needs are very—

MARION   Now you're an expert on what my son needs?

TERESA   I'm not an expert but I did my AQ in special education.

MARION   Fuck, of course you did.

TERESA   He needs to—

MARION   You have no right speaking to anyone about my son with-
            out my consent.

TERESA   Alex is my student. I have a professional obligation—

MARION   To talk to one of us before you decide to just take matters
            into your own hands.

TERESA   I did. Curtis and I...

            Beat.

MARION   What? You what?

TERESA   We discussed it. I didn't just take matters into my own
            hands. He knew I was speaking to Ms. Larson. I wouldn't
            have pursued it without consulting with—

MARION   *(to herself)* This is a fucking nightmare.

TERESA   Alex is making progress. Please don't forget that. I am
            the first person that has actually been able to get through
            to him.

MARION   You are not the first person!

TERESA   I'm the first person here! It's because I have been work-
            ing with Alex during class, after class, at recess, that he's
            finally—

MARION   And do all of your students receive this level of attention,
            Miss Stewart?

TERESA   Alex needs the attention. Other students don't necessarily—

MARION   He needs it or you do?

TERESA   What?

MARION   I'm just asking.

TERESA   Asking what exactly?

MARION   You don't think I know what you're doing?

TERESA   No. I don't, actually.

MARION   The more time you spend with my son, the more contact you're able to have with my husband. Isn't that how you've arranged things?

TERESA   I haven't arranged anything.

MARION   No, the child of the man you're fucking just happens to need more attention than every other student in your class.

TERESA   Alex's progress has absolutely nothing to do with my relationship with Curtis. And yes, for the record, Alex does need—

MARION   It must be so romantic... the two of you lying in bed together... reading poetry to each other... discussing my son's academic—

TERESA   Alex needs to be assessed!

Beat.

MARION   Assessed?

TERESA   Tested.

MARION   I know what assessed means!

TERESA   He needs to be working with the resource program.

MARION   You think you're the first person to suggest that we have Alex tested?

TERESA   No. I know I'm not.

MARION   You're right. You're not!

TERESA   Then why haven't you done anything about it?

MARION   I'm not getting into this with you.

TERESA   Look…

She stops herself.

She looks at MARION.

He's a great kid. He really is. He's smart and funny and clever. But it's only going to get harder for him. I'm sure you know that. If you don't do something about it now… while he's young enough to…

She stops herself.

I know I'm the last person in the world you want to be hearing this from but you need to consider this for him. You need to consider it if you—

MARION   We have. We have considered it.

TERESA   Okay. So...

MARION   I don't want that for him. I don't want him treated differently. I don't want him to be isolated or—

TERESA   Of course you don't.

MARION   I don't want him put into some kind of separate stream or... he's a sensitive kid. He wouldn't handle it well.

TERESA   I wouldn't underestimate him. To be honest... I think he'll be relieved once—

MARION   Relieved?

TERESA   Yes.

MARION   How would any of this be a relief for him?

TERESA   Because these systems work for him. He'll—

MARION   You don't understand.

TERESA   I do.

MARION   You don't. You spend a couple of hours a week with him.

TERESA   I spend forty hours a week with him!

MARION   Because it's your job. You're not with him—

TERESA   Well, from the sounds of it I spend more time with your son than you do!

Beat.

MARION   Excuse me?

TERESA looks at her.

TERESA   It's true. You're never home.

MARION   Because I work, you little cunt.

TERESA   You work evenings, weekends.

MARION   And why do you think that is? For fun? I work for them. Everything I do... everything is for them... for my family. So we can have the life that we have. So we can afford to send Alex here. So I can pay your goddamn salary.

TERESA   You don't pay—

MARION   I would love nothing more than to be at home with my son every night instead of sitting in a fucking open-concept office waiting for some conference call from some asshole in another fucking time zone. I would love to bring Alex to school every morning. I would love to be able to volunteer for class trips...

I hate being away from him… having to work late into the evenings without being able to tuck him in… having to ask him how his day was over the phone. He is my son. Being away from him is one of the hardest things I have to—

TERESA   It hasn't stopped you.

MARION   Stopped me?

TERESA   You're still…

MARION   I am not going to stand here and justify the decisions I… that we have made together… as a family… that enable my son to have the kinds of opportunities that he—

She stops herself.

(to herself) Why am I even going into this with you… you of all fucking people.

TERESA   Because I have seen what Alex is like when he gets the kind of—

MARION   Enough! It's enough already. You don't get to be part of this conversation. You don't get to weigh in on what happens to my son. Do you understand me?

TERESA   His future—

MARION   Has nothing to do with you!

TERESA   I care deeply about Alex.

MARION   If you cared about him, you wouldn't have—

TERESA   I care about him more than you know!

           Beat.

MARION   What does that mean?

TERESA   Nothing.

MARION   No. What the fuck does that mean?

TERESA   Never mind.

           TERESA walks away from her.

MARION   Don't you walk away from me. What did you—

TERESA   My relationship with him is important.

MARION   And?

TERESA   And he's going to be an important part of my life.

MARION   What are you—

TERESA   We're moving in together… Curtis and I.

MARION   Jesus Christ!

TERESA   We were waiting until the end of the school year… until
           Alex is finished.

MARION   You're moving in together?

TERESA   Yes.

> *Beat.*

> *MARION buries her head in her hands.*

MARION   Oh god.

> *After a moment she looks at TERESA.*

> *MARION laughs again.*

Okay…

> *She continues laughing.*

Okay…

> *Beat.*

> *MARION looks at TERESA.*

So… how is this going to work? Will he be moving in with you, because you're sure as hell not taking the house, so… where will you be living?

TERESA   We're figuring that out.

MARION   You're moving in together and you haven't figured out where you'll be living?

TERESA   We haven't made any firm decisions yet.

MARION   Well that says something at least.

TERESA   It doesn't say anything.

MARION   It does, actually. Curtis is usually very good with those sorts of things... those sorts of details. It's sort of a strength of his.

TERESA   What is a strength of his?

MARION   Moving. I've never had the stomach for it. But he... he loves it... the looking, the search for the perfect place, the packing even. So it's just interesting that you haven't talked about it. I would have thought it would be the first thing he would have talked about.

TERESA   We're waiting until the end of the school year to decide.

MARION   Of course you are. And then he'll probably move in with you... in your little apartment... until you find something more comfortable.

TERESA   Probably.

MARION   And will the two of you be living off of your salary or will he be picking up more work... how is that going to sort itself out?

TERESA   We're figuring it out.

       Beat.

MARION   I'm guessing you've never been married before?

TERESA   No. I haven't.

MARION   How many men have you been with?

TERESA   That's not any of your business.

MARION   Have you ever lived with someone? A boyfriend... a partner?

TERESA   I know what I'm getting myself into.

MARION   All right. I just hope you're prepared, that's all. You're going to need more than a goddamn teaching gig to keep the two of you afloat, believe me. We'd be living in the gutter if we—

TERESA   You wouldn't be living in the gutter. You don't have to be so dramatic. You're not the only one contributing at home.

MARION   In our household? Oh yes I am.

TERESA   No, you're not. I know how much each of you makes.

MARION   Oh, you do.

TERESA   Yes. I do. He's told me.

MARION   Has he?

Beat.

Has he also told you how much we've had to borrow from my family over the past three years? How I had to take on a new position at the office with longer hours so we could finally start paying them back?

TERESA   I know things have been tight.

MARION   And how I had to beg him to take on new clients but he still couldn't get his shit together? Did he tell you that?

TERESA   He did. He's told me all of that. He also told me that you're the one who insists on vacationing twice a year and that he's never seen you wear the same pair of shoes twice.

MARION   Oh, go fuck yourself.

TERESA   I know that work has been slow for him. He's looking at his options... maybe changing careers paths.

MARION   You don't just change career paths at his age.

TERESA   He's looking at his options.

MARION   You are so naive it is unbelievable!

TERESA   We will figure it out. Neither of us are concerned about that right now.

MARION   Well of course you're not. Why would you be? Everything is so easy for the two of you, isn't it? You have no obligations, no responsibilities.

You don't have to worry about carpools, or a new refrigerator, or who's taking whose parent to the doctor. You don't have to worry about anything. Right now it's just you and your future. You've got the rest of your lives to figure everything out.

Beat.

That's all going to change... you know that, don't you? This honeymoon of yours will end and eventually you'll be dealing with life... just like the rest of us.

Eventually you'll be left with the dishes and the mortgage and the passing of the newspaper back and forth in the morning without uttering a single fucking word.

MARION looks at TERESA.

If you're actually going to do this... if the two of you are actually going to insist on breaking this family apart, then you deserve each other... and whatever miserable existence you find yourselves living with.

TERESA I'm not trying to break your family apart.

MARION Well that's what's going to happen, isn't it? You're going to rip us apart with your bare hands.

TERESA That's not true—

MARION And if Curtis thinks for one fucking second that he'll have custody of any kind—

TERESA   Curtis is a wonderful father.

MARION   Yeah, well, he's a shitty husband.

TERESA   You don't need to punish him by—

MARION   Trust me... if I wanted to punish him I would do a lot worse. This is for Alex.

TERESA   Alex loves his father.

MARION   And have either of you stopped to consider how he's going to react to this... how he's going to react when he learns that his father is leaving... and not just leaving but leaving to be with his teacher?

TERESA   Alex and I are close.

MARION   You don't think that will change?

TERESA   I know... in time, I think that he'll... I hope that he'll come to...

MARION   This will destroy Alex.

TERESA   I'm prepared to do whatever it takes to make this easy for him.

MARION   He isn't good with other kids.

TERESA   Kids?

MARION   He'll be replaced.

TERESA   No one is replacing anyone.

MARION   And I'm going to be the one who's going to be picking him up off the floor while the two of you start a new life together.

TERESA   He will be a part of that. Alex will be the centre of our lives.

MARION   You say that now.

TERESA   I promise you.

MARION   Curtis always wanted a bigger family.

TERESA   Well… he doesn't. We've talked about it.

MARION   And now that he'll have this young trophy wife.

TERESA   Stop.

MARION   He'll be so thrilled to start over again with you. You'll give him everything he always wanted.

TERESA   That's not true.

MARION   It is. It is true.

TERESA   No. It's not. He knows I can't—

MARION   You'll give him the perfect fucking—

TERESA   I can't have children.

Beat.

MARION   What do you mean you can't? Have you tried or—

TERESA   No. I haven't tried.

MARION   So you've chosen not to—

TERESA   No.

MARION   Then how would you—

TERESA   Because when my uterus was removed it became pretty
            fucking clear that I wasn't going to be having children.

            Beat.

MARION   When did—

TERESA   You know, I don't actually want to talk about this with you.

            Beat.

            TERESA walks to her desk, puts on her sweater, and sits.

            MARION watches her.

            Beat.

MARION   I wasn't even thinking about children at your age.

TERESA   Well, I've been thinking about it my whole life so...

They look at one another.

MARION   *(quietly)* I miscarried.

    Beat.

(quietly) Did he tell you that?

    TERESA shakes her head no.

Twice. The first time I wasn't very far along, but the second time… I had to deliver. It was awful, it…

    She stops herself.

Curtis was heartbroken. That whole period of time…

    She stops herself.

No one tells you that it might be difficult. That it might not happen the way you imagine. You expect that when you want to have a child… you'll be able to. That it will…

    She looks at TERESA

You have options. You can adopt.

TERESA   Would you have adopted?

MARION   We talked about it.

TERESA   And?

MARION   And… Curtis wanted to keep trying. Then we had Alex.

          Beat.

          It's hard, you know… whether you have a child or not…
          it's hard.

TERESA   *(quietly)* Some things make it harder.

MARION   Having a child, it…

          Beat.

          It's the most complicated, wonderful, horrific relationship
          I've ever had.

TERESA   Alex means well.

MARION   Of course he does. He's my baby. He's just…

          MARION stops herself.

          She rubs her eyes. She breathes heavily.

TERESA   Are you all right?

MARION   I think I'm just tired.

          MARION sits at one of the small desks.

          I'm exhausted, actually.

          Beat.

TERESA   Me too.

> *They look at one another.*

> *Beat.*

MARION   Sometimes I just want to be left alone somewhere... far away... where no one can find me.

> *MARION looks off, lost in thought.*

> *TERESA watches her closely.*

TERESA   He knows that.

MARION   What?

TERESA   Curtis. He knows that you want to be left alone.

MARION   I didn't mean literally.

TERESA   Still... he can tell. He can feel that you—

MARION   Being left and being left alone are two very different things.

> *Beat.*

TERESA   He's tried.

MARION   Tried?

TERESA   He's suggested that you see someone together.

MARION   That doesn't constitute trying. The man's just given up.

TERESA   He hasn't given up.

MARION   No?

TERESA   No. He...

She stops herself.

He wants his life to be different.

MARION   We all do. We all want our lives to be different. But that doesn't give him permission to live his life however he wants... to just exit his marriage.

I've had opportunities too, you know... to be with other men. But I would never act on it. I would never do that to him.

The worst part is he hasn't even given me a chance.

TERESA   He has given you a chance.

MARION   No, he hasn't. He has never sat me down and talked to me about it.

TERESA   He has. You don't...

She stops herself.

MARION   What? I don't what?

TERESA   Listen!

MARION   That is not true.

TERESA   He's told me… he has tried to talk to you about it… but you
           change the subject or you leave the room. He's told me…
           you've literally left the room midconversation because he
           brought something up that you didn't want to hear.

MARION   Once. That happened once.

TERESA   Everything has to be your way… all the time.

MARION   I shouldn't have to apologize for having high expectations.

TERESA   You're right. You shouldn't. But if he can't talk to you…
           if you won't listen to him—

MARION   I listen!

TERESA   How is it any kind of partnership if you don't—

MARION   You've never been married. What the hell would you know
           about—

TERESA   I know that if you love someone, if you respect them—

MARION   It's not as easy as just—

TERESA   Are you in love with him?

           Beat.

MARION   That is a very difficult question to answer.

TERESA   Well, it shouldn't be.

MARION   Well... it is.

     Beat.

     When you've lived with someone... when you've known someone as long as we've known each other, it...

     She stops herself.

     We also used to talk all the time. When we first met... when we first started dating... we were inseparable. We couldn't stand being apart from one another. He had this infectious energy. He made me feel like I could do anything. Like anything was possible.

     But you get older... you change and your relationship isn't the way it used to be... and you're not the way you used to be. You don't mean for it to happen. It just does.

     Beat.

     And then you have a child... a family... and everything just...

     Beat.

     I know we've grown distant. I can feel it. I've felt it for a long time now. But I don't... I don't know how to reach him... I don't know how to reach across the table... or the bed even to let him know that I'm still here... that I'm still...

MARION looks at TERESA.

How did you do it?

TERESA   What?

MARION   You found a way to get close to him. What did you do?

TERESA   I didn't do anything.

MARION   You did. You connected to him. How?

TERESA   I don't know. I listened to him.

MARION   And?

TERESA   And what?

MARION   What else?

TERESA   Nothing.

MARION   No. You figured something out.

TERESA   I didn't figure anything out.

MARION   You did.

MARION looks at her.

MARION Give me a way to connect to him. Give me a way to...

MARION goes to the binder.

This... is this what he likes?

TERESA What?

MARION Please. This is my marriage. You've only known each other a couple of months. We've been together for twenty-four years.

TERESA I—

MARION I was there when he got his first job. I was there when his mother died... when our son was born. We have shared an entire lifetime together. I know him in a way that no one else will. Please! Give me a way to—

TERESA Stop! What you're asking me... I don't understand. How can you not know how to connect to your own husband? If you've had so much time together... why has it taken you so long to...

She looks at MARION.

No... it is not my fault that you needed something like this to happen in order for you to see how lucky you are... how lucky you are to have the life that you have.

Curtis has been so good to me. You have no idea what that means.

MARION You care about each other.

TERESA   No. You have no idea what my life has been like. For the past few years… I couldn't be touched. I couldn't let anyone get close to me. I had difficulty leaving my house, I didn't socialize, I had to take a break from teaching. Everything about my life changed.

          Having such a huge part of me… just taken out. Like somebody came along and just scooped everything out. I have this giant hole inside me. I can feel it. When I lie down… when I bend over… there is this huge part of me that is missing.

          He is the first person that I have been able to stand being around. The first person I let into my life… that I can actually talk to about it without—

MARION   Is there no one else you can—

TERESA   Trust me. I've tried to talk to them. I have. But I see that look in their eyes… that glazed look they get if I start talking about it. No one wants to hear about it. No one wants you to talk about it. Everyone wants you to just move on but… I can't. It's all I think about. It consumes me.

          I see women… ordinary women walking down the street… women with their children and I just… I lose it. I break down on the sidewalk. Just seeing a baby carriage, I…

          TERESA buries her head in her hands.

MARION   *(quietly)* I understand.

TERESA   How can you possibly understand?

MARION   I can imagine.

TERESA   You've had a child. I will never be able to...

They kept telling me... they did... at the hospital. They tried to prepare me for it. They told me what they were doing... what they were taking out. That there would be no way for me to...

Beat.

I'm going through menopause. Menopause! It's...

MARION   Can't they give you something?

TERESA   I've tried everything. Nothing works. I'm just so sick of it. The wearing hundreds of layers all the time because I never know when I'm going to be hot or cold... the feeling like I'm crawling out of my skin... the exhaustion... the emptiness. I'm sick of—

A phone rings.

MARION and TERESA are both caught off guard.

MARION rushes to her purse. She pulls out her cellphone and answers it.

MARION   *(into the phone)* Hello?

MARION moves to the far corner of the room.

TERESA moves to her desk, pretending to occupy herself.

(into the phone) Did you… no, no he won't wear those… he doesn't like the way they… the blue ones, in the bottom drawer… I know, I can hear him… no, I'm still at the office… I know… I'm on my way home… no… no, don't put him on the phone, tell him… tell him I'm coming… it's okay, tell him it's… okay, bye.

> *MARION hangs up.*

TERESA   Is everything all right?

> *Beat.*

MARION   It's Alex.

TERESA   Is he—

MARION   I have to get home.

> *MARION goes to collect her things. She puts her coat on.*

> *TERESA watches her.*

TERESA   It was never about you… you know that, don't you?

> *MARION looks at her.*

MARION   And yet… here we are.

TERESA   I know.

> *Beat.*

They look at one another for a long moment.

MARION *heads for the door.*

She stops.

MARION   I...

       Beat.

       (quietly) I wasn't thinking clearly.

TERESA   What?

MARION   What I did.

TERESA   What you did?

       Beat.

MARION   I sent them.

TERESA   Sent what?

MARION   What you wrote... the exchanges... the emails.

TERESA   I don't understand.

MARION   The emails you wrote each other... I sent them to Mr. Williams. I didn't think it through.

TERESA   You... what?

MARION   He's not the only one.

TERESA   What do you mean he's not the only one?

MARION   I sent them to the parents' board.

TERESA   The board?

MARION   The chair... Barbara... she's a family friend.

TERESA   Oh my god.

MARION   I told them to fire you. I told them I'd pull Alex out of the
           school. I said I would make a scene if they didn't get rid
           of you.

TERESA   When did you—

MARION   This morning. I sent them this morning.

TERESA   *(quietly)* No.

MARION   I didn't think it through.

TERESA   You have to fix this.

MARION   How?

TERESA   I don't know. You have to contact them. You have to write
           to them or call them. You have to tell them it isn't—

MARION   What... that it isn't true? It is true.

TERESA   But you... you should have come to me first. Why didn't you come to me first? You could have at least given me a chance to—

MARION   To what?

TERESA   I don't know... to...

She looks at MARION.

This is my job... my income.

MARION   You'll be okay.

TERESA   Okay? You think someone else is going hire me after—

MARION   You're a good teacher.

TERESA   Tell them that! Tell them what you just said to me.

MARION   I don't know what difference it will make.

TERESA   It...

Beat.

I'll go to them myself if I have to. I'll tell them everything... I'll tell them the entire situation. I'll tell them about Curtis... about you coming to see...

TERESA looks at her.

You knew... this entire time. When you first walked in here... you let me... I told you... why would you do something so...

Beat.

Why?

Beat.

MARION   *(quietly)* Because...

Beat.

I didn't want to be the only one in pain.

TERESA   So this... this makes you feel better?

Beat.

MARION   *(quietly)* No.

TERESA looks at her.

TERESA   You know... I have always tried to give you the benefit of the doubt. You...

TERESA turns away.

Get out.

MARION   I didn't mean to—

TERESA   Yes. You did. You did mean to.

MARION   I didn't know what I was doing.

TERESA   You knew exactly what you were doing.

MARION   I didn't—

TERESA   Get out.

        Beat.

MARION   Teresa.

TERESA   Out!

        Beat.

        TERESA turns away.

        MARION looks at her. She opens the door and leaves.

        TERESA looks around the room. She walks to her desk and begins to reorganize things.

        She breathes heavily, trying to contain herself.

        She sees the binder still open on her desk. She takes a moment and then violently pushes it to the floor.

        End of play.

Acknowledgements

They say it takes a village to raise a child. The same is true for a play. There are so many people who helped contribute to the life of this piece and to my growth as a writer throughout the process.

I am forever grateful to the following people:

To Anna Chatterton, Audrey Dwyer, Natasha Greenblatt, Aisha Sasha John, Kaitlyn Riordan, and Meghan Swaby. I had the great fortune of developing the first draft of this play over the course of a year with these tremendous women as part of the Write From the Hip Program. Their questions and insights were instrumental in the early stages of development.

To Philip Akin, Daniel Barbosa, Harmony Cohen, Sascha Cole, Mitchell Cushman, Erin Fleck, Daryl Fridenberg, Mel Hague, Sandra Henderson, Rachel Jamin, Rob Kempson, Camellia Koo, Andrew Kushnir, Jason Mandlowitz, Zachary Mandlowitz, Andy McKim, Emma Mackenzie Hillier, Hannah Moscovitch, Brian Quirt, Sabryn Rock, Anusree Roy, Michael Rubenfeld, Mark Sadowski, Kelly Straughan, Julie Tepperman, Ari Weinberg, Gina Wilkinson, and Aaron Willis. These are the friends, family members, and artists who read drafts of the script, who offered their input, who held my heart when I needed it most, and whose generosity of spirit helped me to write this play.

To Ian Arnold, my literary partner in crime.

To Annie Gibson, Blake Sproule, Mandy Bayrami, and Leah Renihan for the incredible opportunity to have this play live on in print.

To the women at Nightwood Theatre, Denyse Karn, Rebecca Peirson, Laura Pomeroy, and Michelle Alexander, whose work behind the scenes made the initial reading, workshop production, and main stage premiere a success.

To Bonnie Beecher, Richard Feren, and Kelly Wolf, the talented design team who helped to bring the world of this play to life. To Ashley Westlake for keeping us on track and to Rachel Steinberg for her constant care.

To Susan Coyne and Christine Horne, whose bravery, talent, and wisdom were invaluable in the creation of these two characters. Marion and Teresa would not be who they are if not for you.

To Erica Kopyto, who helped me see the light at the end of every tunnel and whose warmth and guidance were a constant inspiration.

To Kelly Thornton, who was the engine that drove this piece to the main stage. Kelly, without your belief in this play and your belief in me... none of this would have been possible.

And to Marcus... for being there every step of the way.

To all of you who helped me tell this story... thank you.

© Will O'Hare

Jordi Mand is a Canadian playwright. Her first full-length play, *Between the Sheets*, premiered in 2012 as part of Nightwood Theatre's '12/'13 season in Toronto and has since been produced both nationally and internationally. Ms. Mand is a resident artist of Theatre Passe Muraille and a past member of Tarragon Theatre's Playwrights Unit. Upcoming projects include new plays with Nightswimming Theatre, Theatre Yes, and UnSpun Theatre. Ms. Mand is a graduate of the National Theatre School of Canada.

First edition: February 2014
Printed and bound in Canada by Imprimerie Gauvin, Gatineau

Cover design and illustration by Leah Renihan
Book design by Blake Sproule

 **PLAYWRIGHTS CANADA PRESS**

202-269 Richmond St. W.
Toronto, ON
M5V 1X1

416.703.0013
info@playwrightscanada.com
www.playwrightscanada.com